ANTON BRUCKN

MESSE E-MOLL

für achtstimmigen gemischten Chor und Bläser

Mass in E minor
for Eight-Part Mixed Chorus and Wind Instruments

Zweite Fassung / Second Version

(1882)

WAB 27

Neuausgabe nach den Quellen von
New edition based on original sources by

Rüdiger Bornhöft

Klavierauszug / Vocal Score

C. F. PETERS

FRANKFURT/M. · LEIPZIG · LONDON · NEW YORK

INHALT / CONTENTS

Vorwort

Noch während der ersten Bauphase des neugotischen Mariä-Empfängnis-Doms in Linz erhielt Anton Bruckner von Bischof Franz Joseph Rudigier im Sommer 1866 den Auftrag, eine Messe zu komponieren. Die *Messe in e-Moll* wurde schon Ende November desselben Jahres fertig gestellt,[1] doch vergingen bis zu ihrer Uraufführung noch rund drei Jahre. Über das bevorstehende Ereignis ließ Bruckner am 13. September 1869 den Wiener Hofkapellmeister Johann Herbeck wissen: „Ich sitze stabil bis mich meine Zeit nach Wien ruft, im Priesterseminar zu Linz, u. plage mich schrecklich mit dem Einstudiren meiner 8 stimmigen Vocal Messe, welche am 29. d[ieses] M[onats] als am Michaelitage hier in Linz zur Einweihung der neuen Domkapelle unter meiner Leitung aufgeführt werden wird."[2] Bruckners Messvertonung fand in der Presse ein überwiegend positives Echo, und das *Linzer Volksblatt* resümierte: „Überblicken wir nun das ganze Werk, so muß jedermann gestehen, daß diese Komposition zu den bedeutendsten der Gegenwart gehört."[3]

Bischof Rudigier war von der ihm gewidmeten Messe so tief beeindruckt, dass er Bruckner ein Sonderhonorar von 200 Gulden zukommen ließ und ihm eine Grabstätte in der Krypta des neuen Doms zusagte. (Diese ehrenvolle Zueignung sollte sich allerdings nicht erfüllen.) Mit euphorischen Worten und der ihm eigenen Devotion bedankte sich der Komponist beim Bischof am 19. Oktober 1869 aus Wien für die Gratifikation: „Eine der höchsten Auszeichnungen ward mir zutheil durch die Dedication an bischöfliche Gnaden von meiner achtstimmigen Consecrationsmesse. Darüber, daß die Widmung so liebevoll angenommen wurde, und daß meine schwachen Leistungen gewürdigt wurden, zu einer so großartigen Feierlichkeit ertönen zu dürfen; darüber wird so lange ich lebe, mein Herz mit Stolz erfüllt bleiben. Ewigen Dank dafür!"[4] Jahre später, in einem Brief vom 18. Mai 1885 an Chordirektor Johann Baptist Burgstaller in Linz, erinnerte sich Bruckner an das denkwürdige Ereignis und schrieb in Bezug auf seine Messe: „1869 von mir einstudirt u. dirigirt an dem herrlichsten meiner Lebenstage bei der Einweihung der Votivkapelle."[5]

Die e-Moll-Messe erklang bei der Linzer Uraufführung in einer 1. Fassung. An ihr nahm Bruckner in den Jahren 1876 und 1882 mehrere Veränderungen vor: er überprüfte die Architektur, den Periodenbau und verbesserte an einigen Stellen die Melodieführung sowie die Instrumentation. Die im Juli 1882 vollendete 2. Fassung des Werkes – sie wird heute allgemein bevorzugt und bildet auch den Gegenstand der vorliegenden Edition – erlebte in Anwesenheit des Komponisten zum Abschluss der Jahrhundertfeier des Linzer Bistums am 4. Oktober 1885 im Alten Dom ihre erste öffentliche Aufführung.[6]

Dem Dirigenten Adalbert Schreyer sandte Bruckner am 28. Oktober 1885 die begeisterten Zeilen: „Aus der Ferne rufe ich Ihnen nochmals meinen innigsten Dank und tiefste Bewunderung zu für die künstlerische Heldenthat der sehr gelungenen Aufführung meiner E Messe! Unauslöschlich wird meine Freude darüber sein!"[7] Am gleichen Tag richtete Bruckner einen Dank auch an den schon erwähnten Chordirektor Burgstaller, wobei er seinem Brief einen quellengeschichtlich bedeutsamen Zettel mit letzten geringfügigen Änderungswünschen zur Messe beifügte.[8]

Die Messe Nr. 2 in e-Moll nimmt unter den drei in Linz entstandenen Messen Bruckners eine gesonderte Stellung ein. Während in den Orchestermessen in d-Moll bzw. f-Moll der klassisch-symphonische Gestus vorherrscht, beruht die Einmaligkeit der e-Moll-Messe auf der Verschmelzung des alten Palestrina-Stils mit der modernen Instrumentenführung des 19. Jahrhunderts. Mit dem Werk gelang es Bruckner auf beispielhafte Weise und mit größter Souveränität, verschiedene Stilarten zu einer künstlerischen Einheit zusammenzufügen. In Klang und Satz ist weitgehend die orchestrale Ausdrucksgestaltung aufgehoben, nicht zuletzt aufgrund der außergewöhnlichen Besetzung: vier- bis achtstimmiger gemischter Chor, begleitet von 15 Holz- und Blechblasinstrumenten (ohne Flöten und Tuba). Diese Klangstruktur bestimmt nachhaltig den Charakter der Komposition.

Das achtstimmige *Kyrie* (e-Moll) ist im Grunde ein A-cappella-Satz, der an nur wenigen Stellen von Hörnern und Posaunen gestützt wird. Ruhige Melodiebögen überlagern sich zu dissonanzreichen Spannungsmomenten und verleihen dem Satz so eine ganz eigentümliche Feierlichkeit. Sein Mittelteil „Christe eleison" (T. 39) führt zur dramatischen Steigerung des Flehrufs und kulminiert vor Wiedereintritt des „Kyrie eleison" (T. 74) in einer Generalpause.

Das nachfolgende *Gloria* (C-Dur) besteht aus einer Art Sonatensatz mit anschließender Fuge. Die phrygische Unisono-Melodie in Sopran und Alt, die als 1. Thema das „Et in terra pax" eröffnet, kehrt später im „Quoniam" (T. 98) als Reprise wieder. Das 2. Thema „Domine Deus" (T. 29) steht, wie im Sonatensatz üblich, in der Dominanttonart; die Durchführung wird aus dem „Qui tollis" (T. 65), einem Andante-Mittelteil, gebildet. Ein vierstimmiges Doppelfugato (T. 133) mit Coda (T. 186) beschließt den Satz.

Machtvoll und affirmativ hebt das *Credo* (C-Dur) mit dem „Patrem omnipotentem" an; Kontraste dazu bilden das introvertierte „Et incarnatus est" (T. 55) und das hymnische „Et resurrexit" (T. 95). Mit dem „Et in Spiritum" (T. 155) wird der Unisono-Beginn reprisenartig wieder aufgenommen. Ungewöhnlich ist das „Et vitam venturi" (T. 211), das abweichend zu vielen anderen Messvertonungen nicht als Fuge, sondern als schlichter Nachsatz komponiert ist.

Im Palestrina-Stil a cappella beginnt das achtstimmige *Sanctus* (G-Dur). Eine ekstatische Steigerung in kanonischer Verdichtung führt zum homophonen Höhepunkt „Dominus Deus" (T. 27). Den Schlussteil bilden „Pleni sunt" (T. 33) und „Hosanna" (T. 40).

Von Chromatik geprägt ist das fünf- bis siebenstimmige *Benedictus* (C-Dur). Das Hauptthema wird vom 1. Horn solistisch vorgestellt, auch der Mittelteil (T. 19) beginnt mit einem Hornsolo. Eine kurze Durchführung des Hauptthemas (T. 44) führt zur Wiederholung (T. 61) mit vertauschten Stimmen. Besondere Erwähnung verdient eine Generalpause, die Bruckner nachträglich aus Gründen der Periodizität und wohl auch als Stilmittel der Kontemplation an den Satzanfang stellte.

Im achtstimmigen *Agnus Dei* (e-Moll) wird das einleitende Unisono-Thema des Chores zweimal variiert aufgegriffen (T. 21 in der Dominanttonart und T. 45) und mündet dann in das „Dona nobis pacem" (T. 53), das mit dem reminiszenzartig wiedereingeführten „Kyrie eleison"-Motiv aus dem ersten Satz (dort T. 75, Sopran II) kontrapunktiert wird.

Die e-Moll-Messe war – ebenso wie die zuvor entstandene d-Moll-Messe – von Bruckner in erster Linie für den liturgischen Gebrauch bestimmt. Darauf weisen die Anfänge des *Gloria* und des *Credo* hin, in denen die vom Vorsänger zu intonierenden Initien traditionsgemäß nicht auskomponiert sind. Bei einer konzertanten Wiedergabe empfiehlt es sich, zu Beginn dieser beiden Sätze die vorgeschlagenen Choralintonationen von Tenor/ Bariton (Solo oder Tutti) anstimmen zu lassen.[9] In der dritten Messe in f-Moll nahm Bruckner von vornherein Rücksicht auf eine Konzertaufführung und integrierte jene Eingangsworte in die Komposition.

Bruckners drei große Messen aus den Jahren 1864 bis 1868 bilden zusammen eine imposante Eingangspforte zu seinen nachfolgenden Monumentalsymphonien, die den eigentlichen Weltruhm des Komponisten begründen. In der Rückschau ragt die e-Moll-Messe durch ihre expressive Modernität als ein einsamer Gipfel der geistlichen Vokalmusik des 19. Jahrhunderts weit heraus.

Ein von Bruckner selbst angefertigter Klavierauszug zur e-Moll-Messe ist nicht überliefert.[10] (Der des Erstdrucks stammt von Cyrill Hynais, veröffentlicht 1896 im Verlag Doblinger, Wien.) Der vorliegende Klavierauszug geht im Wesentlichen auf Kurt Soldans Ausgabe von 1937 zurück.[11] Die Neuausgabe der Partitur (Edition Peters Nr. 10914) gab den Anlass, Soldans Klavierauszug grundlegend zu revidieren und mit der Lesart der Partitur in Übereinstimmung zu bringen; neu und als Hilfe zur Einstudierung wurde der Chorsatz aller A-cappella-Stellen im Kleinstich in den Klavierpart aufgenommen.

Bremen, Dezember 2004   *Rüdiger Bornhöft*

[1] Vgl. Bruckners Bemerkung im Brief vom 2. Dezember 1866 an Rudolf Weinwurm: „Meine Messe 8stimmig, Vocal mit Harmoniebegleitung zur Einweihung der Votiv=Kapelle ist fertig." Zit. nach *Anton Bruckner, Briefe*, Band I, hrsg. von Andrea Harrandt und Otto Schneider †, Wien 1998 (= *Anton Bruckner, Sämtliche Werke*, Bd. 24/1), S. 63. – Zu allen weiteren Ausführungen im Vorwort vgl. auch Michaela Auchmann, *Anton Bruckners Messe Nr. 2 e-Moll (WAB 27): zur musikalischen Gestaltung, Wirkungs- und Rezeptionsgeschichte*, Diss. (mschr.), Wien 1991.

[2] *Bruckner, Briefe I* (wie Anm. 1), S. 111.

[3] *Linzer Volksblatt* vom 9. Oktober 1869, Rezension von Johann Evangelist Habert; zit. nach Claudia Catharina Röthig, *Studien zur Systematik des Schaffens von Anton Bruckner auf der Grundlage zeitgenössischer Berichte und autographer Entwürfe*, Göttingen 1978, S. 70.

[4] *Bruckner, Briefe I* (wie Anm. 1), S. 113.

[5] Ebd., S. 264.

[6] Eine Voraufführung der Messe fand bereits am 26. September 1885 statt. Vgl. dazu Max Auer, *Anton Bruckner als Kirchenmusiker*, Regensburg 1927, S. 215.

[7] *Bruckner, Briefe I* (wie Anm. 1), S. 277.

[8] Vgl. ebd.: „Nochmal schicke ich die Partitur der E Messe, da ich einige Zeichen etc. verändert habe, wie der beiliegende Zettel anzeigt." (Brief vom 28. Oktober 1885 an J. B. Burgstaller).

[9] In der liturgischen Praxis sind bei *Gloria* und *Credo* bis heute verschiedene Intonationen gebräuchlich. Welche von ihnen (und in welcher Weise) bei den genannten Aufführungen der e-Moll-Messe zu Lebzeiten Bruckners verwendet wurden, ist nicht bekannt; die in der vorliegenden Edition mitgeteilten Intonationen sind Vorschläge des Herausgebers, die ohne weiteres ersetzt werden können.

[10] Auskunft über die Quellenlage zur e-Moll-Messe gibt der Revisionsbericht in der Partiturausgabe (Edition Peters Nr. 10914).

[11] Der von Soldan erstellte Klavierauszug erschien 1937 in der Edition Peters als Nr. 4114; nach einer Revision durch Fritz Oberdoerffer wurde die Ausgabe seit 1973 unter der Nr. 8168 weitergeführt.

Preface

In the summer of 1866, while the neo-Gothic Cathedral of the Immaculate Conception in Linz was still under construction, Anton Bruckner received a commission from Bishop Franz Joseph Rudigier to compose a setting of the Mass. By the end of November the *Mass in E minor* was already completed.[1] Some three years were to pass, however, before it was given its first hearing. Bruckner wrote about the impending event to the Viennese court conductor Johann Herbeck on September 13, 1869: "Until my summons to Vienna arrives, I am sitting still in my priests' seminar and tormenting myself horribly by rehearsing my eight-voice Mass, which will be premiered here in Linz under my direction on Michaelmas, the 29th of this month, to inaugurate the new cathedral chapel."[2] Bruckner's Mass was by and large warmly received by the press; the *Linzer Volksblatt* went so far as to say, "Anyone surveying the work in its entirety would have to admit that this is one of the most significant compositions of our time."[3]

Bishop Rudigier was so impressed by the Mass dedicated to him that he had Bruckner paid a special honorarium of 200 gulden and vouchsafed him a burial plot in the crypt of the new cathedral – an honorific promise which, however, was not to materialize. Writing from Vienna on October 19, 1869, Bruckner thanked the bishop in euphoric terms with his inbred obsequiousness: "One of the loftiest distinctions was bestowed upon me by the dedication to Your Grace of my eight-voice Consecration Mass. The fact that the dedication was so lovingly accepted, and that my poor efforts were allowed the honor of being heard at such a magnificent festive occasion, will fill my heart with pride as long as I live. For this I give you my eternal gratitude!"[4] Years later, writing to the choir director Johann Baptist Burgstaller of Linz on May 18, 1885, Bruckner recalled the memorable event: "[My Mass was] rehearsed and conducted by me in 1869 on the most magnificent day of my entire life, to consecrate the votive chapel."[5]

When the E-minor Mass was premiered in Linz it was heard in its first version. Bruckner made several changes to this version in 1876 and 1882: he reviewed its architecture and phrase structure and improved the melodic writing and the instrumentation in several passages. The second version, completed in July 1882, is generally preferred today and forms the basis of the present edition. It received its first public hearing in the composer's presence on October 4, 1885, when it was given in the Old Cathedral at the conclusion of the centennial celebrations for the Linz bishopric.[6]

On October 28, 1885, Bruckner sent the following excited lines to the conductor Adalbert Schreyer: "Crying from the depths, I once again send you my most heartfelt thanks and my deepest admiration for your heroic artistic exploit: the very successful performance of my Mass in E [minor]! My joy at this shall be inextinguishable!"[7] On the same day, Bruckner also expressed his thanks to the aforementioned choir director Burgstaller, enclosing a slip of paper that proves relevant to the work's source tradition as it contains his final minor alterations to the text.[8]

Of the three Mass settings that Bruckner produced in Linz, the Mass no. 2 in E minor occupies a special position. If the orchestral Masses in D minor and F minor are dominated by the ethos of the classical symphony, the uniqueness of the E-minor Mass resides in its blend of the ancient Palestrina style and a modern nine-teenth-century treatment of the instruments. With this work, Bruckner successfully combined several styles in exemplary fashion and with consummate mastery into a unified whole. The expressive orchestral writing has largely been subsumed in the sound and the compositional fabric, not least of all because of the remarkable scoring: a four- to eight-voice mixed chorus accompanied by fifteen wind and brass instruments (without flutes or tuba). These timbral prerequisites left an indelible mark on the character of the entire work.

The eight-voice *Kyrie* (in E minor) is basically an *a cappella* piece supported in a few passages by horns and trombones. Peaceful arcs of melody overlap to form a texture rich in tension and dissonance, lending the movement a solemnity all its own. The middle section, "Christe eleison" (m. 39), leads to a dramatic heightening of the imploration, culminating in a general pause before the recurrence of the "Kyrie eleison" (m. 74).

The next movement, *Gloria* (in C major), consists of a sort of sonata-allegro form followed by a fugue. The "Et in terra pax" opens with a Phrygian *unisono* melody in the sopranos and altos as a first theme which is later recapitulated at "Quoniam" (m. 98). The second theme, "Domine Deus" (m. 29), is set in the dominant, as is customary in sonata form. The *Andante* central section, "Qui tollis" (m. 65), comprises the development, and the movement ends with a four-voice double fugato (m. 133) and coda (m. 186).

The *Credo* (in C major) stands out forcefully and affirmatively, with the "Patrem omnipotentem" contrasting with the introverted "Et incarnatus est" (m. 55) and the hymnic "Et resurrexit" (m. 95). The unisono opening returns in the manner of a recapitulation at "Et in Spiritum" (m. 155). The "Et vitam venturi" (m. 211) is unusual in that, in contrast to many Mass settings, it is composed as an unadorned postlude rather than a fugue.

The eight-voice *Sanctus* (in G major) opens *a cappella* in the Palestrina style. An ecstatic intensification in an increasingly dense canonic texture leads to a homophonic climax at "Dominus Deus" (m. 27). The "Pleni sunt" (m. 33) and "Hosanna" (m. 40) make up the concluding section.

The five- to seven-voice *Benedictus* (in C major) is marked by chromaticism. The principal theme is stated solo by the first horn; the central section also opens with a horn solo (m. 19). A brief development of the principal theme (m. 44) leads to a repeat with parts inverted (m. 61). Special mention should be made of a general pause that Bruckner later inserted at the beginning of the movement, articulating the periodic structure and probably introducing a stylistic element of contemplation.

The eight-voice *Agnus Dei* (in E minor) twice varies the introductory *unisono* theme of the chorus (m. 21, in the dominant, and m. 45). It then leads into the "Dona nobis pacem" (m. 53), which, in the manner of a reminiscence, contrapuntally reintroduces the "Kyrie eleison" motif from the first movement (m. 75 in soprano II).

The E-minor Mass, like its predecessor in D minor, was primarily intended for liturgical use. This is evident in the opening of the *Gloria* and the *Credo*, where, in keeping with tradition, the incipits to be sung by the precentor were not written into the score. In concert performances, it is therefore advisable that the suggested plainchant intonations be sung by solo or choral male voice(s) at the openings of these two movements.[9] In his third Mass, in F minor, Bruckner took the possibility of a concert performance into account from the very outset by integrating these opening words into the fabric of his composition.

All in all, Bruckner's three great settings of the Mass from 1864 to 1868 form an impressive entryway to the monumental symphonies which were to follow and which form the actual basis of his worldwide fame. In retrospect, the E-minor Mass, in its expressive modernity, towers like an isolated mountain peak far above the sacred vocal music of the nineteenth century.

There is no known vocal score of the E-minor Mass prepared by Bruckner himself.[10] (The vocal score of the first edition was the work of Cyrill Hynais and was published by Doblinger of Vienna in 1896.) Our vocal score essentially derives from Kurt Soldan's edition of 1937.[11] The new edition of the full score (Edition Peters No. 10914) gave us an opportunity to thoroughly revise Soldan's vocal score and to harmonize it with the readings in the full score. Further, the choral parts of all *a cappella* passages are now included in the piano part in small print as a rehearsal aid.

Bremen, December 2004

Rüdiger Bornhöft
(Translation: J. Bradford Robinson)

[1] See Bruckner's comment in his letter of December 2, 1866, to Rudolf Weinwurm: "My eight-voice Mass for voices with wind accompaniment for the consecration of the votive chapel is finished." Translated from *Anton Bruckner: Briefe*, i, ed. by Andrea Harrandt and Otto Schneider, *Anton Bruckner: Sämtliche Werke*, xxiv/1 (Vienna, 1998), p. 63. – For all other information in this preface see also Michaela Auchmann: *Anton Bruckners Messe Nr. 2 e-Moll (WAB 27): zur musikalischen Gestaltung, Wirkungs- und Rezeptionsgeschichte*, Diss. (typewritten), Vienna, 1991.

[2] *Bruckner: Briefe*, i (see note 1), p. 111.

[3] Review by Johann Evangelist Habert in *Linzer Volksblatt* (October 9, 1869); see Claudia Catharina Röthig: *Studien zur Systematik des Schaffens von Anton Bruckner auf der Grundlage zeitgenössischer Berichte und autographer Entwürfe* (Göttingen, 1978), p. 70.

[4] *Bruckner: Briefe*, i (see note 1), p. 113.

[5] *ibid.*, p. 264.

[6] An advance performance of the Mass took place on September 26, 1885; see Max Auer: *Anton Bruckner als Kirchenmusiker* (Regensburg, 1927), p. 215.

[7] *Bruckner: Briefe*, i (see note 1), p. 277.

[8] "Once again I am sending you the score of my Mass in E [minor] because I have altered several signs etc., as the enclosed slip indicates." See *ibid.*, letter of October 28, 1885, to J. B. Burgstaller.

[9] To the present day various intonations for the *Gloria* and the *Credo* have been used in church services. It is not known which of them were employed at the above-mentioned performances of the E-minor Mass during Bruckner's lifetime, nor the manner in which they were sung. The intonations reproduced in our edition are editorial suggestions that may be replaced by others at the performers' discretion.

[10] Information on the sources of the E-minor Mass can be found in the editorial notes, included in the full score (Edition Peters No. 10914).

[11] Soldan's vocal score, published in 1937, was assigned no. 4114 in the Peters catalogue. Since 1973, when it was revised by Fritz Oberdoerffer, it has borne the publisher's no. 8168.

BESETZUNG / ORCHESTRATION

2 Oboi – 2 Clarinetti – 2 Fagotti – 4 Corni – 2 Trombe – 3 Tromboni
Coro

Aufführungsdauer / Duration: ca. 40 Min.

Partitur / Full Score EP 10914
Aufführungsmaterial leihweise und käuflich erhältlich
Orchestral material is available for hire and purchase

MESSE E-MOLL

für achtstimmigen gemischten Chor und Bläser

Zweite Fassung (1882)

Anton Bruckner (1824–1896)
Herausgegeben von Rüdiger Bornhöft

Kyrie

Edition Peters Nr. 10915

32461

2

6

Gloria

*) Intonationen zu *Gloria* und *Credo* (S. 19): Vorschläge des Herausgebers / *Editorial suggestions*

14

Credo

22

23

24

26

32461

28

32

34

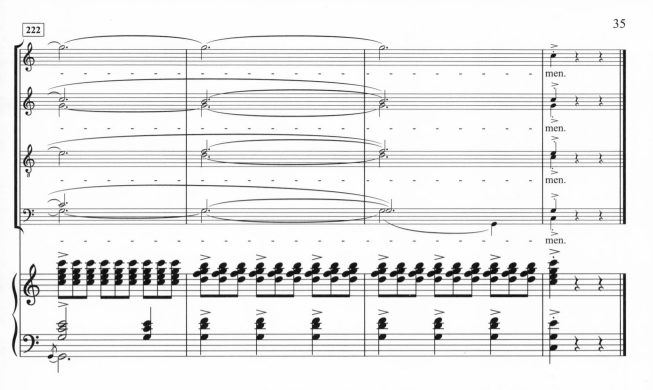

Sanctus

Ruhig, mehr langsam

Anfangs in gemäßigter Stärke, die sich später mehr und mehr steigert.

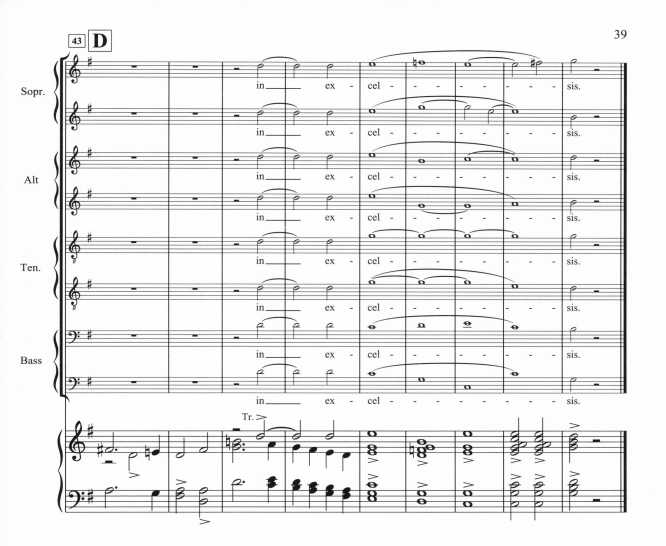

Benedictus

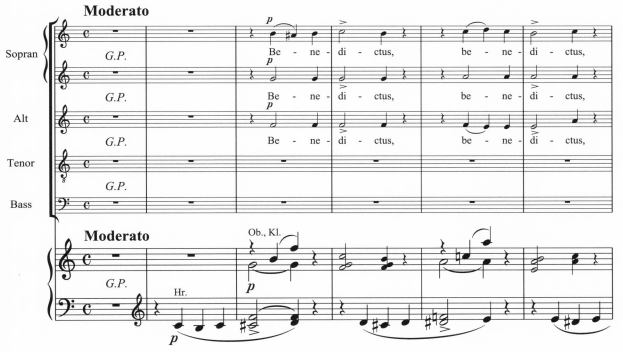

44

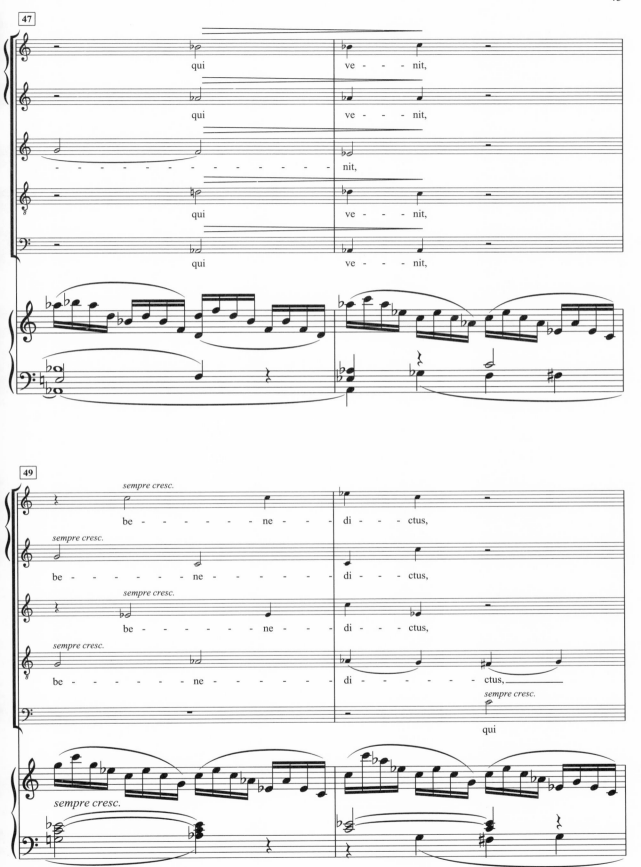

50

Agnus Dei

54

32461

56

EDITION PETERS

Chorsingen – leicht gemacht

CDs zum Lernen der Chorpartien im Selbststudium

JOHANN SEBASTIAN BACH
Johannes-Passion
Klavierauszug EP 8635
CD: MPC 8635-1/2/3/4 (je 2 CDs)

Matthäus-Passion
Klavierauszug EP 4503
CD: MPC 4503-1/2/3/4 (je 2 CDs)

Messe h-Moll
Klavierauszug EP 8736
CD für S1 / S2 / A / T / B:
MPC 8736-11/12/3/4 (je 2 CDs)

Weihnachtsoratorium
Klavierauszug EP 8719
CD: MPC 8719-1/2/3/4 (je 2 CDs)

LUDWIG VAN BEETHOVEN
9. Symphonie / Chorfantasie c-Moll
Klavierauszug 9. Symphonie EP 2227
Klavierauszug Chorfantasie EP 8723
CD: MPC 8723-1/2/3/4

JOHANNES BRAHMS
Ein deutsches Requiem
Klavierauszug EP 3672
CD: MPC 3672-1/2/3/4 (je 2 CDs)

ANTONÍN DVOŘÁK
Stabat Mater
Klavierauszug EP 8639
CD: MPC 8639-1/2/3/4 (je 2 CDs)

GEORG FRIEDRICH HÄNDEL
Der Messias (auf CD gesungen in deutsch)
Klavierauszug EP 4501
CD: MPC 4501-1/2/3/4 (je 2 CDs)

1/2/3/4: 1 = Sopran; 2 = Alt; 3 = Tenor; 4 = Bass

JOSEPH HAYDN
Die Schöpfung
Klavierauszug EP 8998
CD: MPC 66-1/2/3/4

FELIX MENDELSSOHN BARTHOLDY
Elias
Klavierauszug EP 1749
CD: MPC 1749-1/2/3/4 (je 2 CDs)

2. Symphonie (Lobgesang) op. 52
Klavierauszug EP 1750
CD: MPC 1750-1/2/3/4

Die erste Walpurgisnacht op. 60
Klavierauszug EP 1752
CD: MPC 1752-1/2/3/4

WOLFGANG AMADEUS MOZART
Krönungsmesse KV 317
Klavierauszug EP 8115
CD: MPC 8115-1/2/3/4

Requiem KV 626 (Fassung F. Beyer)
Klavierauszug EP 8700
CD: MPC 8700-1/2/3/4

FRANZ SCHUBERT
Messe G-Dur D 167
Klavierauszug EP 1049
CD: MPC 1049-1/2/3/4

GIUSEPPE VERDI
Requiem
Klavierauszug EP 4251
CD: MPC 4251-1/2/3/4 (je 2 CDs)

musicPartner
C. F. Peters · Frankfurt/M.
Leipzig · London · New York
www.edition-peters.de